PHOTOGRAPHERS OF THE WEIMAR REPUBLIC

Stephen B. Jareckie

Worcester Art Museum
Worcester, Massachusetts

Worcester Art Museum
55 Salisbury Street
Worcester, Massachusetts
01609-3196

Library of Congress Catalog Card Number: 86-50508
ISBN: 0-936042-42-7

Production: Anne P. Gibson
Design: Logowitz + Moore Design Associates
Typography: Dix Type Inc.
Printing: LaVigne Press, Inc.

EXHIBITION ITINERARY

Worcester Art Museum
February 2 to March 16, 1986

San Diego Museum of Art
April 5 to May 18, 1986

The Minneapolis Institute of Arts
June 14 to August 10, 1986

Archer M. Huntington Art Gallery, The University of Texas at Austin
October 2 to November 16, 1986

Neuberger Museum, State University of New York at Purchase
February 1 to March 29, 1987

Cover:
Werner Mantz
WILLI OSTERMANN WITH
CARNIVAL CAP, 1928
Silver print
Museum Ludwig, Cologne

ACKNOWLEDGMENTS

Photographers of the Weimar Republic, as an exhibition and as a publication, could not have been brought to completion without the help and support of many persons and organizations.

The Worcester Art Museum is deeply indebted to the National Endowment for the Arts and to the Hall and Kate Peterson Fund for funding in part both the exhibition and this publication. We are grateful to Lufthansa German Airlines for their generosity in providing transportation for loans from Germany. The Andrew W. Mellon Foundation kindly underwrote expenses for research and prepublication costs connnected with this book.

I am personally indebted to the individual curators and their institutions or galleries for sharing their works from the Weimar period with museum viewers and with readers: David Travis, The Art Institute of Chicago; Weston J. Naef and Joan Gallant, The J. Paul Getty Museum; Keith Davis, Hallmark Photographic Collection, Hallmark Cards, Inc.; Colta Ives and Maria Morris Hambourg, The Metropolitan Museum of Art; Clifford S. Ackley, Museum of Fine Arts, Boston; Anne Tucker, Museum of Fine Arts, Houston; John Szarkowski, Susan Kismaric, and Catherine Evans, The Museum of Modern Art, New York; Nancy Barrett, New Orleans Museum of Art; Mr. and Mrs. Eugene Prakapas, Prakapas Gallery, New York; Gerd Sander and Valorie Fisher, Sander Gallery, New York; Van Deren Coke, San Francisco Museum of Modern Art; Roy Flukinger, Harry Ransom Humanities Research Center, The University of Texas at Austin; Daniel Wolf and Bonni Benrubi, Daniel Wolf, Incorporated, New York; Janos Frecot, Berlinische Galerie, Berlin; Ute Eskildsen, Museum Folkwang, Essen; Rudolf Kicken and Suzanne E. Pastor, Rudolf Kicken Galerie, Cologne; and Dr. Reinhold Misselbeck, Museum Ludwig, Cologne.

Many individuals were most helpful to me in the research and promotion of the project: Felix E. Becker, Lufthansa German Airlines, New York; Dr. Bodo von Dewitz and Siegfried Merkel, former curator, Agfa-Gevaert Foto-Historama, Leverkusen; Peter Galassi, The Museum of Modern Art, New York; Malcolm and Sally Gross; Professor L. Fritz Gruber; Manfred Heiting; Robert Flynn Johnson; Dr. Jürgen Kalkbrenner, The Consul General of the Federal Republic of Germany, Boston; Robert Klein, Robert Klein Gallery, Boston; Gordon Lewis; Dr. Eleonore Linsmayer, The Embassy of the Federal

Republic of Germany, Washington, D.C.; Simon Lowinsky; Hattula Moholy-Nagy; Hall Peterson and Jude Peterson; Ernst Renger-Patzsch; Carl Siembab; Robert Sobieszek and Joan Pedzich, International Museum of Photography at George Eastman House; Dr. Christoph Wecker, Goethe House New York; Ann and Jürgen Wilde, Galerie Wilde, Zülpich-Mülheim; Dr. Hans Winterberg and Dr. Anneliese Harding, Goethe Institute Boston.

I would like to thank James A. Welu, director of the Worcester Art Museum, and Tom L. Freudenheim, our former director, for their sustained support of the exhibition from its inception in 1982. Thanks go to the museum staff for the excellent and imaginative way they handled every detail in organizing and presenting *Photographers of the Weimar Republic* at Worcester, in particular: Kathy L. Berg and Cynthia L. Bolshaw, librarians; Kathryn M. Crockett, director of programs and special events; Sally R. Freitag, registrar; Anne P. Gibson, director of publications; Roberta M. Gordon, central services assistant; Sandra Petrie Hachey, photographic services; Virginia I. Harding, supervisor of central services; Martha A. Krom, acting curator of education; James M. Sanders, supervisor of maintenance; Jennifer B. Weininger, director of public information; and Ron White, photographer. Special mention should also be made of former staff members who contributed to the Weimar project: Peter J. Andrews, Gaye L. Brown, Robert C. Coleman, Susan Courtemanche, Brenda M. Negus, Elizabeth A. Page, Roberta Waddell, and Roberta L. Waldo.

Anne Gibson persevered in overseeing the production of this book. Through her editorial and design skills, she saw that *Photographers of the Weimar Republic* will be remembered with an appropriate publication. I am also most grateful to Jean S. Connor for editing the preliminary manuscript and to Dr. Eckhard Bernstein and Corinne B. Green for reading and commenting on the text. Special thanks go to Eveline Heuves from Leiden for her sensitive work in translating German texts that were relevant to the exhibition research, and to my wife, Gretchen K. Fillmore Jareckie, for her help and support. Warm thanks are due Gerd Sander who generously assisted the museum and who strongly supported the project on the conceptual level.

S.B.J.

PREFACE

The Weimar Republic (1919–1933) in Germany witnessed political unrest and its own destruction, but also brilliant artistic achievements. What has survived from the era are family mementos, household furnishings, art, and architecture. Such visual manifestations recall a world that vanished half a century ago. *Photographers of the Weimar Republic* brings together rare photographic prints gathered from a search of collections in the United States and Germany, which help to recreate one of the most dynamic periods of German history.

Images from six leading photographers of the period offer a glimpse of how people lived and created a new environment in Germany in the 1920s. Hugo Erfurth's portraits provide a visual record of Germans who contributed significantly to Weimar culture. August Sander employed his camera to probe the spirit and physical makeup of German society in his monumental project *Menschen des 20. Jahrhunderts (Man of the 20th Century)*. Werner Mantz not only made sensitive portraits of prominent figures in Cologne art circles, but he ably served architects by photographing the new German architecture being built in the Rhineland. Through his New Vision aesthetic, László Moholy-Nagy opened photographers' and viewers' eyes to fresh possibilities in composing pictures of commonplace scenes. Albert Renger-Patzsch, a founder of the *Neue Sachlichkeit* movement, emphasized the beauty in everyday things with simplicity and clarity. Dr. Erich Salomon showed that the newly introduced hand-held Ermanox camera with its large, fast lens could be used to record on film events that shaped the destiny of twentieth-century Europe.

During the 1920s, many artists who had produced works of idyllic romanticism before 1914 and who had experienced the Great War firsthand turned to depicting truth and to creating new means of artistic expression. Artists had a vision for a new Germany. Weimar culture saw the realization of the first, true twentieth-century art forms—especially in architecture, decorative arts, and typography. Photographers benefited from their contact with the new art and established photography as a twentieth-century creative medium. Weimar photographers, like their fellow artists, have exerted profound influence in the post-World War II era on the evolution of twentieth-century aesthetics.

Berlin and cities like Cologne, Dresden, Frankfurt am Main, and Weimar saw intense creative activity during the brief fourteen years of the Weimar Republic. In the 1920s innovative work was accomplished in literature, film, music, architecture, decorative arts, painting, graphic art, and photography, but these achievements were realized in the face of turbulent political and economic conditions. The flowering of the arts in Weimar Germany should therefore be seen within the context of history.

The Weimar Republic was proclaimed on 9 November 1918 by the Social Democratic politician Philipp Scheidemann. Kaiser Wilhelm II had left Germany on the previous day to seek asylum in Holland. On 11 November 1918, the Armistice ending the Great War between Germany and the Allies was signed at Compiègne, France. In the onrush of events, Friedrich Ebert (1871–1925), chairman of the Social Democratic party, was called on to take charge of the newly formed provisional government. Because Scheidemann had proclaimed the republic to prevent Germany from becoming a Soviet state, Ebert felt that his action was irregular; nevertheless, he accepted the responsibility for leadership to save Germany from political chaos.

When the National Constituent Assembly was convened in February 1919 at Weimar, Ebert was elected the first president of the German Republic, generally referred to as the Weimar Republic. Weimar's locale, two hundred kilometers southwest of Berlin, freed politicians from the pressures then existing in Berlin where communists and right-wing militarists perpetrated violence upon political adversaries. Weimar was important as the place where the poet and naturalist, Johann Wolfgang von Goethe, spent most of his life. Goethe had been one of the great humanists one hundred years earlier; hence, it was appropriate to found a republic at Weimar with the hope that Germany would renew her leadership in humanist activities.

Friedrich Ebert and his government confronted grave problems during the early years of the Weimar Republic: the Spartacist attempt to make Germany a Soviet republic; the assassination of the left-wing Spartacist leaders, Rosa Luxemburg and Karl Liebknecht in 1919; the signing of the Treaty of Versailles, which imposed war guilt and heavy reparations on Germany; and the unsuccessful Kapp Putsch to overthrow the government staged by the right-wing extremist, Dr. Wolfgang Kapp in 1920. The government also had to contend with the murder of the Weimar foreign minister, Walther Rathenau, by right-wing militants in 1922; the occupation by the French and the Belgians of the Ruhr in 1923 to speed up tardy reparations payments; the runaway inflation that followed occupation of the Ruhr; and the unsuccessful Munich Putsch in November 1923 led by Adolf Hitler. In 1924 economic conditions stabilized with the implementation of the Dawes Plan, proposed by the American banker and statesman, Charles G. Dawes, which brought about evacuation of the Ruhr, reductions in reparations, and loans to Germany. The Weimar Republic entered a stable period in 1925 that became known as the Golden Twenties and that was to last until the onset of the Great Depression in 1929.

Hugo Erfurth 1874–1948

Hugo Erfurth, who symbolized the Golden Twenties, made superb portraits of painters, architects, and other creative persons who came to his studio in Dresden during the Weimar years.

Born at Halle on the river Saale, Erfurth learned photography as an amateur. After an apprenticeship, he took over at twenty-two the studio of a Dresden court photographer. In 1906 Erfurth moved his family into the Palais Lüttichau, an empire-style mansion on Dresden's fashionable Zinzendorfstrasse, where for the next twenty-eight years he photographed leading citizens and everyday clients.

Not only did customers come to the Palais Lüttichau, but also Dresden artists, who had become Erfurth's close friends, met at the mansion to enjoy each other's company and to discuss the new art movements of the time, such as *Die Brücke* group, which originated in Dresden in 1905. And, of course, they also discussed art photography in Austria and Germany, the Linked Ring in England, and the Photo-Secession in America. Of his work, Erfurth said: ''I owe my guiding principle which I never abandoned, to be true, clear

Hugo Erfurth
HANS THOMA
Oil pigment print
Worcester Art Museum

and authentic and not to mislead myself by fashion and the taste of the time. . . . I preferred to look for faces which showed the marks of fate."[1]

Erfurth greatly admired the Scottish photographer David Octavius Hill, whose aesthetic he applied in his own work: "Hill could see. And through indefatigable observation he raised the technical working process to a creative achievement. He suppressed details in the picture that distracted from making known the characteristics of the head and hands."[2]

From an aesthetic viewpoint, Erfurth was not a revolutionary; he carried over into the 1920s the best German art traditions of the pre-World War I era. His imagery, especially in pictorial structure and psychological impact, reflects German portrait painting of the late nineteenth century, particularly the close-up and half-length studies of realist artists such as the painter Hans Thoma (1839–1924). Thoma, who sat for Erfurth in old age (*fig. 1*), wrote about Erfurth's work: "I am really astonished that it is possible, with the help of photography, to make such deeply psychic portraits."[3]

2
Hugo Erfurth
LOVIS CORINTH, ca. 1920
Oil pigment print
Museum Folkwang, Essen

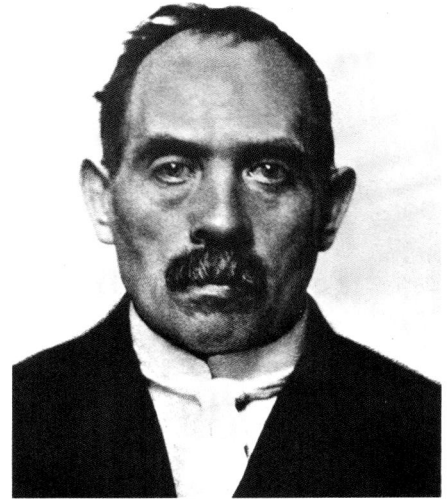

Among Erfurth's most powerful portraits is this moving close-up (*fig. 2*) of the painter Lovis Corinth (1858–1925), taken some time after the artist suffered a stroke in 1911 at fifty-three. The stroke affected Corinth's muscle coordination, but he summoned strength to guide his paintbrush to create evocative pictures during his last years. Corinth, born at Tapiau, East Prussia, studied art at the Königsberg and Munich academies, as well as the Académie Julian at Paris. He fused the best French academism with the German predilection to probe beneath the surface. His later works were in the impressionist and expressionist manners. Corinth probed his own soul through his art as he established the tradition of painting his *Geburtstagporträt* (birthday portrait) in his last years. He witnessed his own physical decline, but not his spiritual decline. Erfurth's empathetic portrait of Corinth shows a man who looks unblinkingly at his destiny and who will not be deterred by circumstances from creating his most important works.

The Dresden artist Otto Dix (1891–1969) and his family were close friends of the Erfurth family. Dix painted portraits of Erfurth, and Erfurth photographed Dix. In one of several studies by Erfurth of the artist in his smock (*fig. 3*), Dix's facial expression reveals the highly intelligent mind of a person used to sizing up people as subjects.

Early in his career Dix was helped by Johanna Ey, who ran a coffee bar in Düsseldorf. Known to the German art world as Mutter Ey (*fig. 4*), she gave support to a generation of modern artists. When the young Otto Dix came to Düsseldorf in 1922, Mutter Ey found him a studio and promoted his art so that within a short time he made a place for himself among Germany's avant-garde painters.

Dix became a leading figure in the *Neue Sachlichkeit* (New Objectivity) movement in which artists depicted German society

3
Hugo Erfurth
OTTO DIX, 1925
Oil pigment print
Museum Folkwang, Essen

4
Hugo Erfurth
MUTTER EY
Silver print
New Orleans Museum of Art
Museum Purchase

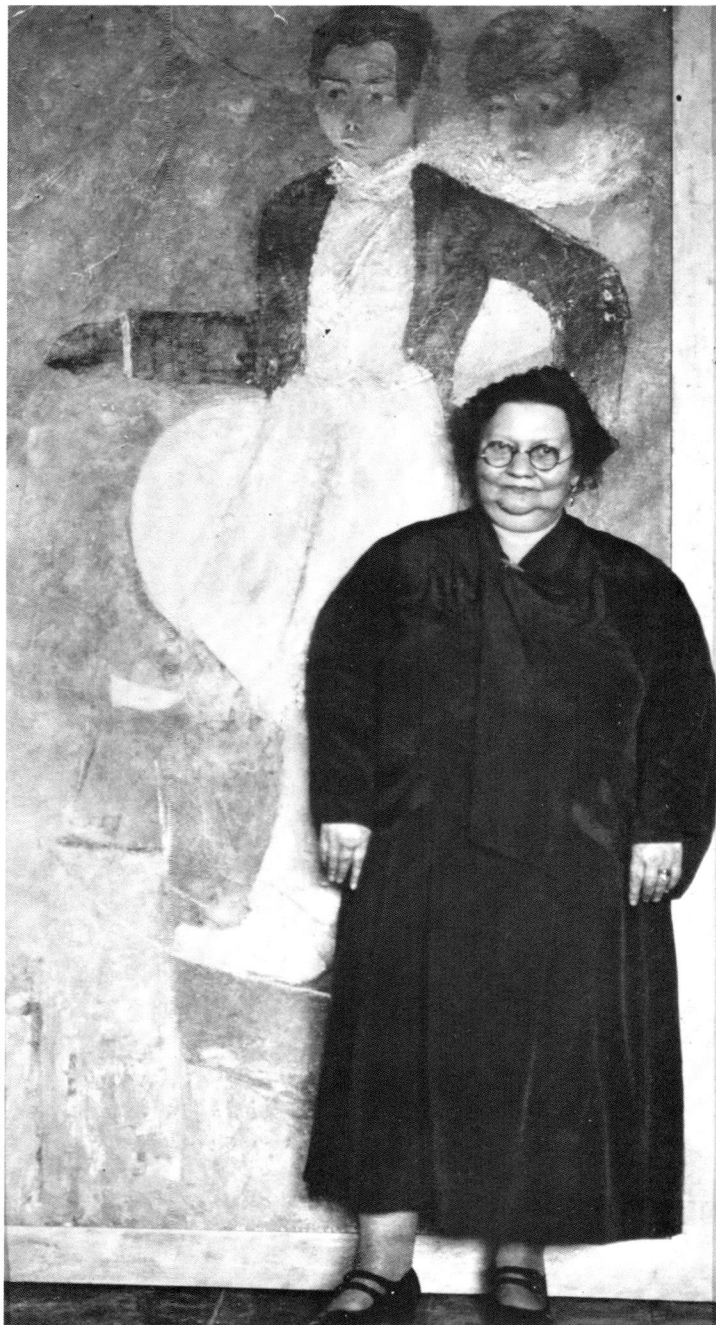

5
Hugo Erfurth
ALFRED FLECHTHEIM,
ca. 1925
Oil pigment print
Museum Folkwang, Essen

with unflinching attention to detail. Otto Dix was forced to leave Dresden when the Nazis created a hostile climate there for artists who did not meet their political standards. Dix and his family went to Lake Constance where he spent his remaining years, to be joined by the Erfurths during World War II.

Alfred Flechtheim (1878–1937) served the art world from 1913 to 1933 as a dealer specializing in the best modern art. He opened his first gallery at Düsseldorf, and was well established in Berlin in the 1920s. His profile fills the frame in Erfurth's photograph (*fig. 5*). The relaxed character of Flechtheim's pose is emphasized by backing his form against the left edge of the picture. The bent middle finger of his left hand firmly holds his cigar. To create his remarkable portraits, Erfurth evolved a technique that gave his work consistency. He posed his subjects in the natural light that passed through the 3.5-meter high windows of the three stately rooms that served as studio space in the Palais Lüttichau. Moveable horizontal curtains, one dark blue and the other white, were often used to modify light falling on a subject's face. On winter after-noons, Erfurth employed arc lamps for illuminating his sitters.

Erfurth preferred to use a stand camera, equipped with a Tessar lens with a 36-centimeter focal length. The rosewood camera, built to his specifications by Herbst and Firl at Görlitz, utilized 9-by-12-centimeter plates, the artist's favorite format. Erfurth had two other cameras that used the same format, a second studio camera with a 25-centimeter f/3.5 Tessar lens, and a hand-held reflex camera.

6

Hugo Erfurth
WALTER GROPIUS, ca. 1927
Silver print
The University of Texas at Austin
Harry Ransom Humanities Research Center
The Gernsheim Collection

Erfurth made camera exposures of his sitters in a straightforward manner on Agfa Ultra plates, but he chose the oil pigment process, a highly creative hand method introduced in 1904, to produce his finished portraits. The oil pigment process suited Erfurth's artistic temperament. The process, which required skillful handling essentially involved bringing out the picture by brushing oil pigment or fatty ink on a gelatin-relief image that had been placed by photographic means on the paper surface. High relief areas (highlights) rejected the pigment or ink while low relief areas accepted the paint work. Thus, Erfurth combined hand skills with photographic technology to produce powerful imagery.

Erfurth's portrait of Walter Gropius (1833–1969, *fig. 6*), founder of the Bauhaus, captures the commanding presence of the architect whose form fills the picture. Gropius, who had witnessed the chaos in Germany at the end of World War I, resoved to find new ways to reconstruct the country. He had trained before the war under the architect Peter Behrens who believed that modern buildings must be clean and orderly structures. Gropius established the Bauhaus in 1919 at Weimar by merging two grand-ducal schools, an academy of art and a school of applied arts. He assembled a group of brilliant artists to teach there including Josef Albers, Marcel Breuer, Lyonel Feininger, Wassily Kandinsky, Paul Klee, László Moholy-Nagy, and Oskar Schlemmer. In 1925 he built a new school of steel and glass at Dessau. Gropius wrote in a Bauhaus manifesto: "Architects, painters, and sculptors must once again recognize and grasp the multiform shape of the building in its totality and its parts. . . . We must all turn back to craft. . . . The artist is the craftsman in his highest form."[4] Bauhaus students were taught to master architecture, decorative arts, and commercial design problems.

7

Hugo Erfurth
THEODOR DÄUBLER, ca. 1930
Silver print
The University of Texas at Austin
Harry Ransom Humanities Research Center
The Gernsheim Collection

The *Dichter* (poet, writer) has always been important to German culture. Goethe and Schiller moved Germans in the nineteenth century just as poets like Däubler and Gerhart Hauptmann have similarly exerted influence in this century. Distinguished by a flowing beard and a large frame, Theodor Däubler (1876–1934, *fig. 7*) also had a large appetite to sustain himself. Born in Trieste, Däubler led a wandering life, traveling to Italy, Germany, France, Greece, and the Orient. His major work was a visionary epic cycle *Das Nordlicht* (*The Northern Lights,* 1910). The sun was the symbol of the spirit for Däubler, and Apollo was for him a link in reconciling Christianity and paganism. *Attic Sonnets* was one of his works from the 1920s.

With the ascendency of the Nazis, Erfurth moved to Cologne in 1934 since his clients at that time came mainly from the Rhineland. When his home was bombed in 1943, Erfurth went to Lake Constance. He was a member of the German Photographic Society from its founding in 1919 until his death in 1948. His portraits, made with artistic integrity, constitute a record of individuals who led their nation.

August Sander 1876–1964

The Westerwald, a district on the east side of the Rhine, was always important to August Sander. Born at Herdorf, a village in the northeast corner of the Westerwald, Sander felt close to the people, the rolling farmland, and the forests of the region, and he refreshed his spirit in the Siebengebirge (Seven Mountains) that overlook the Rhine.

At thirteen Sander started out as a miner's apprentice in an iron mine at Herdorf. By chance he was asked one day in 1892 to guide a photographer from nearby Siegen who wanted to take views from the mine property, and when Sander saw the valley scene before him in the camera's viewer, he resolved to become a photographer. After fulfilling his military obligation, he sought professional photographic training. In 1902 he bought a studio at Linz, Austria, and married Anna Seitenmacher of Trier. Eight years later Sander moved his family to Cologne and set up a studio in the suburb of Lindenthal. In the brochure announcing the studio opening, he wrote that he was concerned with creating ''natural portraits that show the subjects in an environment corresponding to their own individuality, portraits that claim to be evaluated as works of art.''[5] Customers were few initially since the Cologne public sensed that Sander would not provide them with the kind of portraits they were accustomed to commissioning— portraits that placed subjects in contrived studio settings and were retouched to flatter patrons.

To gain additional income, Sander took his camera out of the studio and into the Westerwald to photograph the farming people he knew from his youth. At this time Sander formed the idea for his life study of German society to be called *Menschen des 20. Jahrhunderts* (*Man of the 20th Century*), which would consume his energy during the Weimar years. He began by photographing the farmers, as he believed they were closest to nature and the foundation of society. Sander's portraits of country folk taken between 1910 and 1914 became his archetypes or *Stamm-Mappe,* intended as the introduction to *Menschen des 20. Jahrhunderts.*

Sander ardently admired Goethe and, through photographs, endeavored to create an organic view of man and nature such as Goethe advocated. Also, Sander was interested in ideas about physiognomy put forward by the eighteenth-century Swiss pastor, Johann Kaspar Lavater, who believed that man's inner character shapes his exterior features. Following the concept of the sixteenth-century *Ständebüch (Book of Trades)* in which people were illustrated by rank and vocation, Sander ordered subjects in *Menschen des 20. Jahrhunderts* to represent his view of contemporary society. He began with farmers and continued to laborers, management, professional people, artists, the family, and to those outside of conventional society—circus performers, the unemployed, the blind, and the aged. He pursued his study of twentieth-century man until he was stopped by the Nazis in the early 1930s.

In his pre-1914 photographs, men and women posed in their Sunday clothes holding Bibles, giving their camera images serious and austere formality. The farming people, whose portraits were made in the Weimar period, are seen outdoors in everyday clothes in more relaxed poses. A father and his son (*fig. 8*), dressed in work clothes, took time from their daily routines

8
August Sander
FATHER AND SON,
WESTERWALD, 1931
Silver print
The Museum of Modern Art, New York
Gift of the Photographer

9
August Sander
COUNTRY BARBER STANDING
IN DOORWAY, 1930
Silver print
Copyright of the August Sander Archives
Courtesy of Sander Gallery, Inc., NYC

to have their picture taken under a shade tree. The younger man, perhaps in his sixties, is an active farmer, while his father, who might be in his eighties, deservedly relaxes in his wicker chair (his hands reflect strength and a capability for work).

Following the farmers in Sander's scheme are the artisans, workers, technicians, and industrialists. Among the hand workers is a barber standing before a half-timbered building waiting for his next customer (fig. 9). He wears a traditional white coat, a wing collar, and a necktie that is off center. A folded razor is in his hand while a comb and scissors are kept ready in his breast pocket. At the top of management is the industrialist, Arnold von Guillaume of Cologne, attired in a pin stripe suit (fig. 10). He sits in profile on a Louis XVI armchair. With the exception of the gilt Central European setting, the sitter with his appearance and manner could well be taken for an industrialist from any other Western country.

Among Sander's pictures of professional people is a study of a military student from Cologne (fig. 11) who poses with his sword. He is a member of a Nuremberg student corps and of a fraternity, judging

August Sander
BUSINESS MAGNATE (ARNOLD
VON GUILLAUME), COLOGNE, 1928
Silver print
The Museum of Modern Art, New York
Gift of the Photographer

from the initiation scars on his face. This image as well as the portrait of Arnold von Guillaume was among sixty reproduced in *Antlitz der Zeit (Face of Our Time)* published in 1929 by Transmere Verlag, Munich, to promote the *Menschen des 20. Jahrhunderts* project. The introduction for *Antlitz der Zeit* was provided by Alfred Döblin, author of the novel *Berlin Alexanderplatz*. Döblin concluded: ''The photographs, the expression of this philosopher [Sander], each speak for themselves and together in their order they speak more elegantly than I can do.''[6]

Sander established friendships with artists in Cologne in the early twenties and had close ties with members of the Progressives, a socialist artist's group, including Heinrich Hoerle, Anton Räderscheidt, and Franz Wilhelm Seiwert. Artists often met at Sander's home for goulash, drink, and discussion about art and Weimar politics. Seiwert helped Sander on an important aesthetic matter by pointing out that glossy paper, which Sander used to give clarity and detail to architectural and industrial photographs, was a better choice for printing portraits than the mat surface paper preferred by

August Sander
MEMBER OF A STUDENT SOCIETY
FROM NUREMBERG, 1928
Silver print
The Museum of Modern Art, New York
Gift of the Photographer

12

August Sander
PAINTER HEINRICH HOERLE
DRAWING A PORTRAIT OF
HEIN DOMGÖRGEN, ca. 1927
Silver print
Worcester Art Museum
Mrs. Albert W. Rice Acquisitions Fund

photographers at the time. Sander adopted the use of glossy paper exclusively for his *Menschen des 20. Jahrhunderts* project, as the resulting images had greater sharpness and immediacy.

Sander's portrait of his friend, the painter Heinrich Hoerle (1895–1935) was one of his favorites; it hung in his studio's finishing room. In another image (*fig. 12*), the side of Heinrich Hoerle's face appears in an unusual close-up (enlarged from a section of a photograph of Hoerle at work), which shows him in the act of creating a portrait drawing of a boxer. The subject of this picture within a picture is Hein Domgörgen, one of Germany's well-known European middleweight champions.

A section of Sander's *Menschen des 20. Jahrhunderts* was reserved for husbands and wives, the family, and women—those who form the basis for society and its regeneration. The compositional structure in the portrait of the architect Hans Heinz Lüttgen and his wife is strengthened by placing the subjects close to one another and by repeating line and form (*fig. 13*). The white edge of the woman's scarf follows the line of her husband's shoulder. Her soft, classic features contrast with her husband's rough-hewn face. His eyes reveal the sensitivity that links their relationship and hold the viewer's attention. Young women dressed for an important event (*fig. 14*) posed for Sander in a woodland setting. One is left to wonder about the sort of occasion the young people were celebrating that required a photographer.

Sander photographed street life in Cologne. One of his best-known urban pictures (*fig. 15*) was taken in 1925 when Paul von Hindenburg, the newly elected second president of the Weimar Republic, visited Cologne. (Hindenburg was elected Reichspräsident after Friedrich Ebert's death in April 1925.) To take Hindenburg's picture, Sander set up his camera at a suitable place along the presidential

13
August Sander
THE ARCHITECT HANS HEINZ LÜTTGEN
AND HIS WIFE, COLOGNE, 1928
Silver print
Copyright of the August Sander Archives
Courtesy of Sander Gallery, Inc., NYC

14
August Sander
FARM GIRLS, 1925
Silver print
The J. Paul Getty Museum

15
August Sander
PRESIDENT VON HINDENBURG
AND THE MAYOR OF COLOGNE,
KONRAD ADENAUER, 1925
Silver print
The J. Paul Getty Museum

16
August Sander
AGE, SICKNESS, AND DEATH,
1932
Silver print
The Museum of Modern Art, New York
Gift of the Photographer

motor route and made his one exposure of President von Hindenburg and Konrad Adenauer, Lord Mayor of Cologne, as their open car passed before his lens. The twin spires of Cologne Cathedral rise in the distance making the photograph's locale unmistakable.

Dr. Konrad Adenauer (1876–1967), who wears a top hat in this picture, was Lord Mayor of Cologne from 1917 to 1933 and later served as the first chancellor of the Federal Republic of Germany from 1949 until 1963. Adenauer was tough minded and governed firmly in Cologne and in Bonn. In Cologne he built new port facilities, established a green belt, provided sports grounds, and promoted expositions. As chancellor, he created close ties with the United States, achieved reconciliation with France, and made West Germany an equal among the European powers.

The final group in Sander's study is called the *Letzte Menschen* (last men) and includes the blind, malformed, and disfigured, the aged and the dying. An old man wearing a visored cap and a muffler (*fig. 16*) steadies himself with canes in a dirt street in a Westerwald village. This man faces his last years with courage. Sander's study of twentieth-century German society ends in the Westerwald where it began.

In 1927 Sander wrote as part of his credo: "We must be able to endure seeing the truth, but above all we should pass it on to our fellow men and to posterity, whether it be favorable or unfavorable for us. . . . Therefore, let me speak the truth in all honesty about our age and the people of our age."[7]

Werner Mantz 1902–1983

Like August Sander, Werner Mantz was well known in Cologne in the 1920s. He began taking photographs at fourteen after he bought a hand-held camera at a photo shop on the Hohe Strasse (High Street) in his native Cologne. Initially he photographed old Cologne and the Bergisch Land, countryside east of the Rhine. In 1918 he documented the arrival of the British occupation troops, and in 1920 he recorded a disastrous flood in Cologne.

In 1921 Werner Mantz set up his studio in his parents' house in Cologne, following study at the Bavarian State Academy for Photography in Munich. He began his career by making portraits of Cologne's

leading citizens and by photographing paintings and sculptures by city artists. For portraiture, Mantz chose the 18-by-24-centimeter format because he believed that photographs produced in this size had the optimum scale for reproduction in publications.

Willi Ostermann (1876–1936, *cover*) is seen here in his carnival costume after he had had his nose straightened by cosmetic surgery. In business, Ostermann was a book printer, but in the realm of pleasure, he was the best-known poet and singer of Cologne's famous pre-Lenten carnivals. Besides his carnival songs, he was noted for songs about Cologne and the Rhine. Ostermann expressed a sentiment in one of his last songs that is shared by Cologne citizens who have left their city but yearn to return: "Ich mööcht zo Foss noh Kölle gon (I'd fain walk all the way to Cologne)."[8]

Wilhelm Riphahn (1889–1963) was a leading practitioner of the new international architectural style in Germany. Mantz's portrait of the architect (*fig. 17*) shows him in a characteristic pose with a cigarette hanging from his lips. With the encouragement of Riphahn, Mantz changed the emphasis of his work from

portraiture to architecture in 1926. He received his first architectural commission from Riphahn to photograph the new Cologne hair-dressing salon, Pickenhahn. Riphahn, who designed the Pickenhahn shop, set up his office in the same building. Through Riphahn, Mantz met other architects and enjoyed seven prosperous years photographing architecture until the Depression curtailed work in the Rhineland. The Sünnerterrasse, an elegant and popular restaurant on the east side of the Rhine, was designed by architects Wilhelm Riphahn and Caspar Maria Grod. Mantz emphasized the geometric character of the new German architecture (*fig. 18*) by creating an illusion of pure perspective in which the viewer's eyes are led up to the vanishing point at the far end of the dining room. Beyond the window can be seen the Hohenzollern Bridge, a great arched span that carries the main rail line across the Rhine at Cologne.

Through Riphahn, Mantz received work from the Council for Public Housing Construction, founded in Cologne in 1913. It was one of the leading organizations in Germany concerned with providing imaginative public housing. Because Mantz's

17
Werner Mantz
WILHELM RIPHAHN, ca. 1926
Silver print
Museum Ludwig, Cologne

Werner Mantz

RESTAURANT INTERIOR, SÜNNERTERRASSE,
KÖLN-DEUTZ, 1928
Silver print
Worcester Art Museum
Mrs. Albert W. Rice Acquisitions Fund

pictures were generally made for architect's records, his interior scenes are without people, and details, like furnishings, are shown in perfect order. This unusual Mantz photograph (*fig. 19*) shows an interior space that is lived in; the table is set for coffee. One woman prepares food while the other takes advantage of the bright daylight to embroider.

Mantz photographed store windows. He made a number of pictures to promote Electrola products, and in this photograph (*fig. 20*), Mantz confined his attention to the display itself. The store dummy, in an attitude of studying a score, has been placed in the display to sell the products and to engage the shopper's attention. The sign at the lower left translates: "Enjoyable recollection in the home through Electrola opera and concert series." In the record cabinet behind the mannequin are appropriate albums—a Bach mass, Beethoven symphonies, a Schubert trio, and Verdi's *La Traviata.*

For the architect Bruno Paul, Mantz made exterior and interior views of the Sinn Department Store in Gelsenkirchen, an industrial city near Essen in the Ruhr. In this exterior view, with the ground floor display windows featuring women's fashions (*fig. 21*), Mantz used a diagonal perspective to emphasize the curving glass front of the building.

The design of the Kaufhaus Sinn reflects the influence of Berlin architect Eric Mendelsohn. Like Gropius, he believed that postwar architecture should make a new beginning. Mendelsohn thought of buildings as sculptural forms. He created handsome, utilitarian designs, giving his department stores elegantly curved fronts.

Civil engineering projects appealed to Mantz. This picture of a new highway bridge (*fig. 22)*, believed to be part of an early autobahn connecting Cologne to Bonn, is a compelling example of Mantz's work. The photograph has perfect perspective with the road passing under the bridge towards a vanishing point on the horizon. The sky, with swiftly moving clouds, gives the scene a surreal aspect.

When economic conditions in the early 1930s curtailed construction, Mantz established a studio at Maastricht, The Netherlands, where he specialized in children's portraits from 1932 until his retirement in 1971. Before his death in 1983

19
Werner Mantz
WOMEN IN KITCHEN, 1929
Silver print
Prakapas Gallery, New York

20
Werner Mantz
ELECTROLA SHOP WINDOW,
COLOGNE, 1927
Silver print
The J. Paul Getty Museum

Werner Mantz
KAUFHAUS SINN,
GELSENKIRCHEN, 1928
Silver print
The J. Paul Getty Museum

22
Werner Mantz
BRIDGE (COLOGNE), 1927,
FROM THE PORTFOLIO
WERNER MANTZ:
10 PHOTOGRAPHIEN
1927–1935, 1977
Silver print
San Francisco Museum of Modern Art
Mrs. Ferdinand C. Smith Fund Purchase

Mantz saw that his photographs entered the Museum Ludwig collection. His handsomely detailed images provide a record of the newly created environment during the Weimar period.

László Moholy-Nagy   1895–1946
László Moholy-Nagy was a dominant photographic figure in Weimar Germany. He excelled in creating cameraless photograms, in examining the mores of society through his photomontages, and in evolving new ways to make straight photographic images of what intrigued him in the objective world. Moholy thought of himself as an amateur; in fact, he exhibited as an amateur in the *Deutsche Photographische Ausstellung* (German photography exhibition) at Frankfurt in 1926. Though he viewed photography as one of the arts, he regarded himself as a painter.

Born in Bácbarsòd, Hungary, Moholy was raised by his uncle after his father emigrated to America early in the boy's life. Moholy began his law studies at Budapest, but when World War I broke out, he became an artillery officer in the Austro-Hungarian Army. In 1915 he produced his first drawings and watercolors while recuperating from a concussion. His interest in pursuing an art career led him to Berlin in 1920 where he met Lucia Schultz, an art history student, whom he married in 1921. In 1922 Galerie Der Sturm in Berlin gave Moholy his first one-man show, and he made his first photograms. From 1923 to 1928 he taught at the Bauhaus and edited Bauhaus books. In 1925 he made his first camera images employing his New Vision aesthetic, depicting the world in abstract, diagonal compositions. Moholy's intent was to extend people's vision through photography.

In his Bauhaus book *Malerei, Photographie, Film* (*Painting, Photography, Film,* 1925) he declared: ''The camera can perfect or supplement our own optical instrument, namely the eye. This principle has already been applied to various forms of scientific investigation, such as the study of movement (walking, jumping, galloping) and zoological, botanical and mineral forms (enlargement and microscopic views); but these were isolated experiments and their interconnection was not observed. . . . So far we have only used the camera's potentialities in a secondary

23

László Moholy-Nagy
LUCIA MOHOLY-NAGY AT
BELLE-ILE-EN-MER
Silver print
Prakapas Gallery, New York

manner. . . . This is also seen in so-called mistaken shots—from above, below, or sideways—which already in casual photographs of today are impressive."[9] Thus may be observed Moholy's thought process as he turned his interest to representational camera photography.

Moholy took his first camera images when he and his wife traveled to Paris in 1925. During the summer of that year he experimented further with camera photography when he and Lucia vacationed with the art historian, Sigfried Giedion, and his wife at Belle-Ile-en-Mer off the coast of Brittany. Later Giedion wrote: "I remember a holiday spent together on Belle-Ile-en-Mer where Moholy, deliberately ignoring the usual standpoint of a photographer, took shots looking up from below and looking down from above. The surprising foreshortenings and plunging lines were, only a few years later, to find universal favour as being artistically attractive."[10] Moholy had initiated the practice of using vacation trips for making what appeared to be snapshots, or holiday pictures, of places that he visited. The subject of this enlargement (*fig. 23*) is the artist's wife, who has been photographed combing her hair. It is the study of a female figure, however, rather than a portrait of an individual person. Her firm arms and legs take on an angled, formal structure as she is seen in contrast to the visually soft, changing character of a sandy beach.

Moholy climbed high into the rigging to take a birds'-eye view of a vessel under

24
László Moholy-Nagy
UNTITLED
Silver print
The Art Institute of Chicago
The Julien Levy Collection
Special Photography Acquisitions Fund

full sail (*fig. 24*). Because his camera is pointed straight down, the woman on deck appears to be standing when she is actually lying down. At the top of the frame the viewer is given a glimpse of a person climbing the rope ladder just below the photographer.

Moholy applied the "counter-composition" scheme in which diagonals form the main compositional lines giving dynamism to his photographic work. (In 1925 Dutch artist Theo van Doesberg had evolved the diagonal-composition principal as an alternative to Piet Mondrian's static, rectangular pictorial structure.) In this picture of a house painter at work in an upper story window (*fig. 25*), Moholy utilized the converging angles of the power lines and the roof edge to draw the eye upward to the lone worker at the top of the picture frame. The figure appears to float in space, seen against the glare of brilliant sunlight.

Inspired by Russian artist Aleksandr Rodchenko's black ground linocuts of 1918 and by his own work with photograms and woodcuts in the early 1920s, Moholy turned to creating negative prints after he began to do representational photography. Through negative photographic imagery, he studied the relationship of white against black. Moholy's undated close-up portrait of his wife Lucia was produced in both positive and negative versions. The subtle detailing that is obscure in shadow in the positive version is clearly made visible in this negative print (*fig. 26*).

25
László Moholy-Nagy
PAINTER AT WORK,
SWITZERLAND, 1925
Silver print
Museum of Fine Arts, Boston
Charles Amos Cummings Fund

26
László Moholy-Nagy
UNTITLED (FACE)
Negative print
The Metropolitan Museum of Art
Warner Communications, Inc. Purchase Fund,
1981

In 1928 Moholy ended his teaching association with the Bauhaus at Dessau and moved to Berlin where he established himself as a commercial designer. This straight-down view (*fig. 27*), taken from the Berlin Radio Tower in winter, is a classic example of his post-Bauhaus work. The ground-level details have become pure, geometric shapes, having lost their representational character due to the camera's high vantage point.

Following separation from his wife Lucia in 1929, Moholy traveled to Marseille to make a motion picture, *Marseille Vieux Port.* While he was there, he photographed the port's bridges and harbor. He also took this picture of a busy street through a grillwork (*fig. 28*). The resulting photograph of the Rue Cannebierre conveys the atmospheric character of southern France where the Mediterranean sun washes out details.

For taking camera photographs Moholy preferred to use a 6-by-9-centimeter Ernemann plate camera. However, when he later made pictures for his book *Street Markets of London* (1936), he used a 35-millimeter Leica, which made him less intrusive to his subjects.

Moholy assisted the Deutsche Werkbund, an arts-and-crafts organization, in arranging the New Vision exhibition, *Film und Foto,* held at Stuttgart in 1929. More than a thousand photographs were included in this major avant-garde showing. The exhibition was international in scope and among the Americans represented were Berenice Abbott, Imogen Cunningham, Andreas Feininger, his brother T. Lux Feininger, Paul Outerbridge, Man Ray, Charles Sheeler, Edward Steichen, Ralph Steiner, Edward Weston, and his son Brett. Edward Weston wrote about American viewpoints in the catalogue. Among the European photographic artists were André Kertész, Piet Zwart, Hannah Höch, Kurt Schwitters, Hugo Erfurth, and

László Moholy-Nagy
VIEW FROM THE RADIO TOWER, BERLIN, 1928
Silver print
The University of Texas at Austin
Harry Ransom Humanities Research Center
The Gernsheim Collection

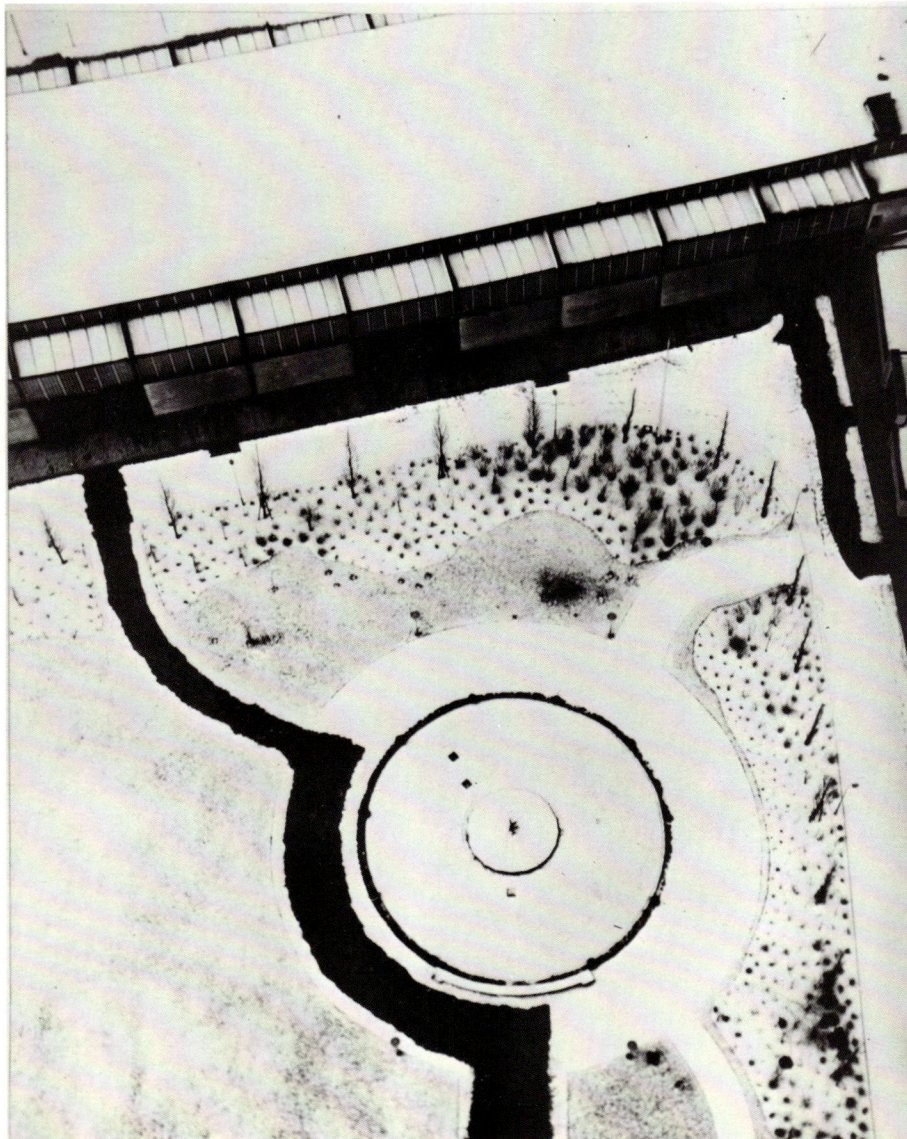

Albert Renger-Patzsch. The exhibition revealed that many photographers were working along similar tracks, but were evolving their ideas independently. The prints in *Film und Foto* reflected similar attitudes in making matter-of-fact, sharply detailed images.

With Hitler's coming to power, Moholy left Germany, going first to Amsterdam in 1934 and then to London in 1935. He followed Walter Gropius to the United States where he settled in Chicago. There Moholy founded the School of Design, which eventually became part of the Illinois Institute of Technology. He devoted his last years to his students and to writing. After his death from leukemia in 1946, Moholy's last book, *Vision in Motion,* was published in 1947.

Albert Renger-Patzsch   1897–1966

In 1927 László Moholy-Nagy and Albert Renger-Patzsch both wrote about their different viewpoints of photography in the German photographic annual *Das Deutsche Lichtbild.* Moholy wrote about photography's place among the visual arts and about using the medium to extend visual perception. Renger-Patzsch, who

28
László Moholy-Nagy
MARSEILLE, 1929
Silver print
Hallmark Photographic Collection
Hallmark Cards, Inc., Kansas City, Missouri

believed that it was unnecessary to explore new photographic techniques, stated in the annual that photography has its own technique with its own clarity and truthfulness in recording subject matter. He wrote: "The secret of a good photograph—which like a work of art may possess aesthetic qualities—is its realism. . . . Let us therefore leave art to artists and endeavor to create photography which will last because of its photographic quality, because its uniquely photographic property hasn't been borrowed from another art."[11]

Albert Renger-Patzsch, who became a leader of the New Objectivity movement in Germany in the 1920s, took up photography in a very natural way by absorbing his father's enthusiasm for the medium. Born in Würzburg in 1897, the twelve-year-old Renger-Patzsch learned the rudiments of taking pictures from his father, who was an amateur photographer and a professional musician. Following army service, Renger-Patzsch studied chemistry at the Dresden Technical College. In 1922 he became head of the picture department of the Folkwang art publishing firm at Hagen, a city to the east of Essen. In

1925 he established himself as a professional photographer at Bad Harzburg, a spa and tourist town in central Germany.

The year 1925 saw the culmination of his early professional activity with the holding of an exhibition at Bad Harzburg and with the publication of his first book, *Das Chorgestühl von Cappenberg* (*The Choir Stalls of Cappenberg*), in which he presented images of organic, man-made forms. Prior to 1925 Renger-Patzsch had devoted his personal work to taking close-ups of flowers and objects. His photograph of a potter's hands (*fig. 29*), dated 1925, comes from his early and fully developed aesthetic; the subject has been presented with simple directness and the hands and the wheel have been rendered with a high degree of tactile quality and realism.

Renger-Patzsch's ideas and work in 1925 were part of the New Objectivity spirit in the arts. The New Objectivity movement, called *Neue Sachlichkeit,* was given its name by Gustav Hartlaub, director of the Mannheim Art Gallery, who exhibited work in 1925 by several German painters, including Otto Dix and Georg Grosz, who had turned to realism in reaction to

29
Albert Renger-Patzsch
POTTER'S HANDS, 1925
Silver print
The Museum of Modern Art, New York
Gift of the Photographer

expressionism. The movement extended its activities to photography and to film-making. A compelling photograph of a fisherman seated in his boat between a lowered sail and a coil of rope (*fig. 30*) presumably relates to Renger-Patzsch's *Die Halligen* (*The Islands of Schleswig-Holstein*), a photographic study of life along the North Sea published in 1927.

Renger-Patzsch also wrote in the 1927 issue of *Das Deutsche Lichtbild* that the photograph is a reliable tool for portraying "impressions which people feel before nature—of plants, of animals, before the works of the architect and the sculptor, before creations of the engineer and the technician."[12] He emphasized the fact that photography should be valued as a medium for showing beauty in materials and structure and that photography is the "absolute master" in conveying with precision such spatial characteristics as height and depth.

Renger-Patzsch's early photographic activities culminated in 1928 with the publication by Kurt Wolff Verlag, Munich, of *Die Welt ist schön* (*The World is Beautiful*), a book of one hundred photographs. The photographer wanted to call his book *Die Dinge* (things) since he viewed it as "a model book of objects and things."[13] The publisher felt that such a title would not promote sales; hence the title for which the book is so well known was adopted.

Die Welt ist schön was published when Renger-Patzsch was thirty-one. He saw the book "as an alphabet intended to demonstrate how pictorial problems can be solved by purely photographic means."[14] The Lübeck art historian Dr. Carl Georg Heise wrote in the book's preface: "Whether we admit it or not, the fact that the world is beautiful is a precondition for art of all kinds. . . . Photographs, however, assuming that they are as vital, bold and creative as those of Albert Renger-Patzsch, have the ability of enriching a far larger circle of people . . . and uniting them in enthusiasm similar to that aroused by the painting of our time. . . . The fact remains that the world of these photographs is beautiful."[15]

Agave (*fig. 31*), one of the plant studies in *Die Welt ist schön,* represents the photographer's early work in which he concerned himself with close-ups. In this study, the camera has been moved up so that only the essential part of the plant fills

30
Albert Renger-Patzsch
MAN IN BOAT, 1927
Silver print
The University of Texas at Austin
Harry Ransom Humanities Research Center
The Gernsheim Collection

31
Albert Renger-Patzsch
A G A V E ,   1 9 2 4
Silver print
The University of Texas at Austin
Harry Ransom Humanities Research Center
The Gernsheim Collection

32
Albert Renger-Patzsch
PORTRAIT, 1927
Silver print
The University of Texas at Austin
Harry Ransom Humanities Research Center
The Gernsheim Collection

the frame. Dr. Heise wrote about Renger-Patzsch's botanical work: ''The plant is depicted in its typical beauty and, at the same time, extended into lineal ornamentation of fascinating tension, without losing anything of its own natural essence.''[16]

This close-up of a young woman from the Halligen Islands (*fig. 32*) also appears in *Die Welt ist schön.* She has been presented with simple directness. Although it is not intended as a psychological study, the young woman's trusting and strong character, tempered by a harsh environment, emanates from the picture. Renger-Patzsch's well-ordered view of what makes up the world was completed in *Die Welt ist schön* with studies of animals, landscape, materials, architecture, technology, and symbols of twentieth-century culture.

Renger-Patzsch believed that actual color was not required in representing a subject in photography and that the black-and-white medium was fully capable of translating the color, atmosphere, and textural nuances of a scene. He clearly applied this viewpoint in photographing a winter landscape (*fig. 33*) with its soft, atmospheric light of a gray day.

In Renger-Patzsch's view, machines are no less beautiful than nature or works of art. In this photograph of Lübeck, a north German port (*fig. 34*), he utilized the dark masses of the harbor cranes to create through repetition a unified composition. This was one of eighty images to be reproduced in *Lübeck,* another book published by Renger-Patzsch in 1928.

That same year Renger-Patzsch moved to Essen where he became associated with the Museum Folkwang. He became the institution's photographer, and in exchange for making documentary photographs of the museum's collection, he was provided with studio and laboratory space to pursue his own work.

Albert Renger-Patzsch
UNTITLED, ca. 1932
Silver print
The Museum of Fine Arts, Houston
Museum purchase with funds provided by
Mr. and Mrs. Harry B. Gordon

34
Albert Renger-Patzsch
DOCKSIDE CRANES
Silver print
The J. Paul Getty Museum

Albert Renger-Patzsch
STREET IN ESSEN AT THE
TRAIN STATION, 1930
Silver print
The Museum of Modern Art, New York
Gift of the Photographer

At Essen Renger-Patzsch embarked on a project not previously attempted—making a comprehensive study of Germany's industrial heartland, known as the Ruhrgebiet. In America Edward Weston had photographed Armco Steel in Ohio in 1922, and Charles Sheeler had been commissioned by the Ford Motor Company in 1927 to photograph the River Rouge Plant. For eight years Renger-Patzsch photographed aspects of the Ruhr in all seasons—the factories, pitheads, rail lines, streets, housing, farm land, and pure landscape.

Essen, situated at the heart of the Ruhr, has a history that goes back to the ninth century when a convent was founded by the Benedictines. When Friedrich Krupp established his steel firm in Essen in 1811, the Ruhr was a farming area and a hunting preserve. At the beginning of this century, Essen emerged as a center for heavy industry in a coal and steel region located to the north of the Ruhr, the river that flows into the Rhine at Duisburg. At the center of Essen, Renger-Patzsch photographed the masonry embankment with its great round arches (*fig. 35*) on which the main rail line passes through the city. Passersby in this picture, taken near the main railway station, provide the view with a sense of scale.

To accomplish his photographic work, Renger-Patzsch preferred the 9-by-12-centimeter format. In his monograph Fritz Kempe quoted Renger-Patzsch: "I work only with 9x12 cameras—a mirror reflex for photographs of animals and children and a folding camera for all other purposes. I use lenses of varying focal lengths, most of them between 8 and 30 cm, and I prefer a restricted transmitting power to huge lumps of glass. . . . I only use small-format cameras to photograph my children on holiday by the sea. I leave the developing and printing to the photo dealer, and I refrain from giving him any good advice on the subject."[17]

Renger-Patzsch remained in Essen until 1944 when his residence and a large part of his archives were destroyed by bombing. He moved afterward to Wamel in Westphalia, east of the Ruhr district, where he spent the rest of his life.

In 1957 the Gesellschaft Deutscher Lichtbildner (German Photographic Society) awarded the David Octavius Hill Medal to Renger-Patzsch on his sixtieth birthday. The citation read: "We honor the pioneer of modern German photography, which owes to him its maturity and honesty. At the same time, we recognize a life's work of exemplary unity, rigid discipline and uncompromising conviction."[18]

Dr. Erich Salomon   1886–1944

Dr. Erich Salomon's mirror portrait of himself with two companions in evening dress (*fig. 36*) is indicative of a man who chose to blend into the environments in which he photographed. The reflected image also illustrates his working methods as a photojournalist (*Bildjournalist*), an occupational title that he, himself, coined. The picture was taken in existing light (without flash) with a tripod-mounted Ermanox camera that had been introduced three years previously in 1925. This photograph dates from 1928, the year Salomon achieved international fame when his haunting pictures, taken through a hole in a bowler hat, of the murder trial of the safecracker Johann Hein were published in the Ullstein magazine *Berliner Illustrirte Zeitung*.

To cover the Hein trial, Salomon hired a taxi to take him four hundred kilometers from Berlin to Coburg, in southern Germany where Hein, who was accused of killing three policemen, was being tried. Photography was forbidden in the courtroom, and Salomon later recounted his experience with court attendants: "When

36
Dr. Erich Salomon
EVENING COMPANY AND
SELF-PORTRAIT, ca. 1928
Silver print
Museum Folkwang, Essen

they realized what was happening, they wanted to confiscate my negatives. But I remembered that old lizard's trick—putting what is useless into the mouth of the enemy—and gave them only a few unexposed plates.''[19]

Though Salomon began his career in photography in an unexpected way, he was superbly prepared—with a background in social customs, language, legal skills, and natural inventiveness—to establish himself as the foremost historian with a camera of his time.

Born into affluent circumstances in Berlin, Erich Salomon had every advantage at the start of his life as his father was a banker and a member of the Berlin stock exchange. The German-Jewish family moved in Berlin society. Erich Salomon pursued varied interests as a young man —beginning with the study of biology, followed by his taking a degree in civil engineering. After working at the Schwartzkopff locomotive plant in Berlin, he went on, at the urging of his parents, to study law at Munich and then at Rostock where he received his doctorate in 1913.

When World War I came, he entered the German Army and was taken prisoner by the French in September 1914 at the first Battle of the Marne, the point where the Germans made their deepest penetration into France. During his four years as a prisoner-of-war, Salomon worked as an interpreter and thereby became proficient in the French language.

In the twenties, after his return to civilian life, his family lost their money in the rampant inflation of the period. Erich Salomon worked for a time at the stock exchange. This was followed by employment in a piano factory and later by ownership of an electric car and motorcycle rental agency. In the motor trade, he not only drove clients around, but en route he also gave them legal advice on tax matters. When his rental business declined as gasoline became plentiful, Salomon went to work in the promotional department at the Ullstein publishing house, where he became an amateur photographer.

Until the mid-twenties, photographers relied on cumbersome hand-held and tripod-mounted cameras and on the magnesium flash apparatus to document public figures for news stories. The utilization of such equipment inevitably produced stiff, posed pictures. People in public life shied away from the resulting unfavorable coverage in the press. The introduction in 1925 of two available light cameras, the Ermanox and the Leica, were a boon to men like Dr. Erich Salomon.

Salomon saw that the Ermanox could be used to make unposed pictures in existing light; thus in the late twenties he proceeded to employ the Ermanox both as a hand-held instrument and a tripod-mounted camera. Flash equipment was not required for the Ermanox because the camera had a fast f/2 or f/1.8 Ernostar lens. The camera, made by the Ernemann Photo-Kino-Werke in Dresden, utilized 4.5-by-6-centimeter glass plates that had to be loaded and exposed one at a time. Salomon employed the most light-sensitive plates available in the twenties, the Ortho Isod plates, rated at 23 degrees Scheiner (equal to ASA 12). Publication prints were enlarged from the small glass negatives. In order to draw less attention to himself and to put his subjects at ease, he often mounted his Ermanox on a tripod and waited until the right psychological moment to trip his shutter, which he did by a long cable release from a position fifteen feet away.

Berlin provided the setting for Salomon's earliest photographs. People were drawn to Berlin in the twenties. The Czech-born editor, Willy Haas, stated in *Die literarische Welt:* ''To become a Berliner—that came quickly, if one only breathed in the air of Berlin with a deep breath. . . . I loved the rapid quick-witted reply of the Berlin woman above everything, the keen, clear reaction of the Berlin audience in the theater, in the cabaret, on the street and in the café . . . that lovely, dry, cool and yet not cold atmosphere, the indescribable dynamic, the love for work, the enterprise, the readiness to take hard blows—and go on living.''[20]

Into this highly charged atmosphere Salomon plunged with the zest of a Berliner. Because he had been so successful with his first photographic efforts, Salomon left his position at Ullstein in 1928 to become a free-lance photojournalist. His picture of the Poetry Section of the Prussian Academy of Arts (*fig. 37*) was taken during his first year of self-employment. Around baize-covered tables, with such accoutrements as ash trays and a telephone, are seated Weimar Germany's

37
Dr. Erich Salomon
MEETING OF THE POETRY SECTION
OF THE PRUSSIAN ACADEMY
OF ARTS IN BERLIN, 1929
Silver print
Berlinische Galerie, Berlin

leading literary figures—Alfred Döblin, Thomas Mann, Ricarda Huch, Bernhard Kellermann, Hermann Stehr, Alfred Mombert, and Eduard Stucken. Döblin, who had written the introduction to August Sander's book *Antlitz der Zeit,* was well known for his work *Berlin Alexanderplatz.* Thomas Mann, one of Germany's foremost novelists, wrote *Buddenbrooks* for which he received the Nobel Prize, and a novel about death, *Der Zauberberg* (*The Magic Mountain*).

Alfred Kerr (1867–1948, *fig. 38*), who presents the viewer with a quizzical expression, looked at German theater with a highly critical mind. Walter Laqueur wrote in *Weimar: A Cultural History* that "Kerr would damn most young playwrights with a pen dipped in acid."[21] He misunderstood Bertolt Brecht who adapted John Gay's eighteenth-century play, *The Beggar's Opera,* to create his brilliant satire about bourgeois society, *The Threepenny Opera.* Alfred Kerr also opposed Max Reinhardt, the showman and impresario who presented expressionist spectacles at the Grosses Schauspielhaus in the early twenties. Kerr, who completed his doctorate at Halle, established himself before 1914 as a critic for such journals as the *Neue Rundschau* (*New Review*) and the *Frankfurter Zeitung.* He admired Henrik Ibsen, George Bernard Shaw, and Gerhart Hauptmann. Kerr left Germany in 1933 on the sixteenth day after the Nazis came to power. He returned to Germany after World War II and died in Berlin at the beginning of a lecture tour in 1948.

In 1930 Erich Salomon stayed nine months in the United States at the invitation of *Fortune* magazine. He spent time in California where he photographed the German actress Marlene Dietrich, who was in Hollywood to act in a Josef von Sternberg film. The sultry actress became a star through her performance in *The Blue Angel* (1930), made by Von Sternberg in Germany and based on a satiric story by Thomas Mann's brother Heinrich. Salomon made a series of shots of Dietrich calling her daughter at four in the morning via the first transatlantic telephone cable (*fig. 39*).

Women engaged in an animated after dinner conversation became subjects for Salomon at a public place in Berlin (*fig. 40*). Two of them happened to be politicians— Katharina von Kardorff-Oheimb, who leans across the table, and Ada Schmidt-

38
Dr. Erich Salomon
DR. ALFRED KERR, BERLIN
THEATER CRITIC, ca. 1928
Silver print
Berlinische Galerie, Berlin

39
Dr. Erich Salomon
MARLENE DIETRICH
TELEPHONING FROM
HOLLYWOOD TO HER
DAUGHTER IN BERLIN,
1930
Silver print
The University of Texas at Austin
Harry Ransom Humanities Research Center
The Gernsheim Collection

Dr. Erich Salomon
TWO FEMALE POLITICIANS,
KATHARINA VON KARDORFF-
OHEIMB AND ADA SCHMIDT-
BEIL, BERLIN, 1930
Silver print
Berlinische Galerie, Berlin

Beil, who faces their two companions. Katharina von Kardorff-Oheimb (1879–1962) supported women's rights in the Weimar Republic and during the post-World War II years. As a member of Stresemann's People's party, she was the first woman to enter the Reichstag, where she served as a deputy from 1920 until 1924. Dr. Gustav Stresemann (1878–1929), a highly intelligent and dedicated statesman, was chancellor of the Weimar Republic for a brief time in 1923 and served as foreign minister in seven cabinets until his death six years later. A tireless champion for reconciliation with France and Russia, he succeeded in making Germany a viable member of the European community. Gustav Stresemann succeeded so well that he was awarded the Nobel Peace Prize in 1926.

Salomon covered the 1929 state visit to Berlin of King Fuad of Egypt. During the visit Salomon photographed the Egyptian king and President Paul von Hindenburg and their entourages in their box at the Berlin State Opera (*fig. 41*). Some of the guests in adjacent boxes, who momentarily forgot their manners, stared with curiosity at the presidential party. Hindenburg and those in his box knew their roles and gave the occasion the dignity it required. Paul von Hindenburg (1847–1934) was elected second president of the Weimar Republic after the death in 1925 of President Friedrich Ebert. Hindenburg, who came from a Prussian military family, served his country in the army from the 1860s until the end of the Great War when as a field marshal he commanded all German land forces. Hindenburg carried the grandeur of the Wilhelmian monarchy over into the Weimar Republic, as Salomon's image clearly demonstrates. Though a monarchist in spirit, once in office, Hindenburg served the Republic conscientiously as president and upheld the constitution in trying times.

The garden of the chancellor's palace in Berlin was the setting for a meeting, on a warm summer's day in 1930, of Dr. Heinrich Brüning's cabinet. Brüning, a financial and economic expert, was the leader of the Catholic Center party. He headed a coalition government from March 1930 to May 1932. Salomon captured the serious nature of a group of men (*fig. 42*) who, in coats and ties, were trying to get some fresh air and, at the same time, grapple

Dr. Erich Salomon
GALA PERFORMANCE AT THE
BERLIN STATE OPERA: KING
FUAD OF EGYPT AND PRESIDENT
VON HINDENBURG, 1929
Silver print
Berlinische Galerie, Berlin

42
Dr. Erich Salomon
BRÜNING CABINET MEETING IN THE
GARDEN OF THE CHANCELLOR'S
PALACE, BERLIN, 1930
Silver print
Berlinische Galerie, Berlin

with Germany's severe economic situation, a situation fueled by unemployment and worldwide depression. When this picture was taken, Germany was without a parliament, and the country was being run by decree for the first time under Article 48 of the Weimar Constitution. Brüning had dissolved the Reichstag in July 1930, and the new Reichstag would not convene until after elections the following September. Seated on the far side of the table in Salomon's picture are: Dr. Schiele (right hand in motion), minister of food; Dr. Wirth, minister of interior; Dr. Dietrich, vice-chancellor and finance minister; Chancellor Brüning (left hand to chin); and Dr. Punder, state secretary of the chancellery. Both white lawn chairs and indoor chairs were used for the meeting.

Three years later, Dr. Erich Salomon and his family moved to The Hague in The Netherlands after Hitler had secured his power. Salomon continued to work as a photojournalist in England and on the continent through the thirties. He considered going to America, but he waited too long and was trapped in Holland when the Nazis invaded the country in May 1940. Salomon, his wife, and younger son Dirk died at Auschwitz in 1944. His son Peter survived World War II and has preserved and promoted his father's work.

To many thinking people the Weimar Republic died on 14 September 1930, when the National Socialist German Workers' Party was firmly established through the nation's parliamentary elections, by increasing its seats in the Reichstag from twelve to one hundred seven. Through political maneuvers, Dr. Brüning continued to serve as chancellor until his government fell on 30 May 1932. Succeeding governments suffered the same fate, and on 30 January 1933 President Paul von Hindenburg named Adolf Hitler chancellor. The burning of the Reichstag on 27 February 1933 gave Hitler the pretext to seize power and, with the death of Hindenburg in 1934, he gained absolute political control in Germany.

NOTES

1 Bernd Lohse, ed., *Hugo Erfurth 1874–1948: Der Fotograf der Goldenen Zwanziger Jahre* (Seebruck am Chiemsee: Heering-Verlag, 1977), 7.

2 *Ibid.*, 7.

3 This statement by Hans Thoma is translated by the author from the text for a gallery label pertaining to Hugo Erfurth in the Agfa-Gevaert Foto-Historama, Leverkusen.

4 Peter Gay, *Weimar Culture: The Outsider as Insider* (1968; reprint, Westport, Connecticut: Greenwood Press, 1981), 98.

5 Robert Kramer, *August Sander: Photographs of an Epoch 1904–1959* (Millerton, New York: Aperture, 1980), 17.

6 Alfred Döblin, "Introduction to August Sander," *Antlitz der Zeit* (1929), in *Germany: The New Photography 1927–33,* ed. David Mellor (London: Arts Council of Great Britain, 1978), 58.

7 Kramer, back cover.

8 C. Harald Harlinghausen and Hartmuth Merleker, *Germany,* 2nd ed. (Geneva: Nagel Publishers, 1965), 426.

9 This quotation has been adapted by Herbert Molderings, "Urbanism and Technological Utopianism: Thoughts on the Photography of *Neue Sachlichkeit* and the Bauhaus" (1978), in Mellor, 89.

10 Andreas Haus, *Moholy-Nagy: Photographs & Photograms,* trans. Frederic Samson (New York: Pantheon Books; London: Thames and Hudson, 1980), 34.

11 Albert Renger-Patzsch, "Ziele," *Das Deutsche Lichtbild* (1927), borrowed and translated by Ute Eskildsen, "Exhibits: Innovative Photography in Germany Between the Wars," in *Avant-Garde Photography in Germany: 1919–1939* (San Francisco: San Francisco Museum of Modern Art, 1980), 40.

12 Albert Renger-Patzsch, "Ziele," *Das Deutsche Lichtbild* (1927), in *Film und Foto: der zwanziger Jahre,* ed. Ute Eskildsen and Jan-Christopher Horak (Stuttgart: Württembergischer Kunstverein, 1979), 95.

13 Fritz Kempe and Carl Georg Heise, *Albert Renger-Patzsch: 100 Photographs* (Cologne and Boston: Shürmann & Kicken Books, 1979), 7.

14 Ute Eskildsen, "Photography and the *Neue Sachlichkeit* Movement" (1978), in Mellor, 105.

15 Kempe and Heise, 9, 10.

16 *Ibid.*, 10.

17 *Ibid.*, 16.

18 *Ibid.*, 18.

19 Han de Vries and Peter Hunter-Salomon, *Erich Salomon: Portrait of an Age,* trans. Sheila Tobia (New York: Macmillan Company; London: Collier-Macmillan, 1967), x.

20 Gay, 128, 129.

21 Walter Laqueur, *Weimar: A Cultural History 1918–1933* (New York: G.P. Putnam's Sons, 1974), 229.

BACKGROUND BOOKS

Fletcher, Banister. *A History of Architecture: On the Comparative Method.* 17th ed., rev. R.A. Cordingly. London: University of London, 1961.

Gay, Peter. *Weimar Culture: The Outsider as Insider.* 1968. Reprint. Westport, Connecticut: Greenwood Press, 1981.

Laqueur, Walter. *Weimar: A Cultural History 1918–1933.* New York: G.P. Putnam's Sons, 1974.

Myers, Bernard S. *The German Expressionists: A Generation in Revolt.* New York: Frederick A. Praeger, 1966.

Richards, J.M. *An Introduction to Modern Architecture.* Harmondsworth, England: Penguin Books, 1940. Rev. ed. 1956.

Von Eckardt, Wolf. *Eric Mendelsohn,* in *The Masters of World Architecture.* Gen. ed. William Alex. New York: George Braziller, Inc., 1960.

Willett, John. *The Weimar Years: A Culture Cut Short.* New York: Abbeville Press; London: Thames and Hudson, 1984.

GENERAL PHOTOGRAPHIC BOOKS

Brockhaus, Christoph, Reinhold Misselbeck, and **L. Fritz Gruber.** *Sammlung Gruber: Photographie des 20. Jahrhunderts.* Cologne: Museum Ludwig, c. 1984.

Coke, Van Deren, Ute Eskildsen, and **Bernd Lohse.** *Avant-Garde Photography in Germany 1919–1939.* San Francisco: San Francisco Museum of Modern Art, 1980.

Coke, Van Deren. *Avant-Garde Photography in Germany, 1919–1939.* First Amer. ed. New York: Pantheon Books, 1982.

de Maré, Eric. *Photography.* Harmondsworth, England: Penguin Books, 1962.

Eskildsen, Ute, and **Jan-Christopher Horak, eds.** *Film und Foto: der zwanziger Jahre.* Stuttgart: Württembergischer Kunstverein, 1979.

Gernsheim, Helmut. *Creative Photography: Aesthetic Trends 1839–1960.* Boston: Boston Book & Art Shop, 1962.

Gernsheim, Helmut, and **Alison Gernsheim.** *A Concise History of Photography.* New York: Grosset & Dunlap; London: Thames and Hudson, 1965.

Gidal, Tim N. *Modern Photojournalism: Origin and Evolution, 1910–1933.* Trans. Maureen Oberli-Turner. Vol. 1 in *Photography: Men and Movements.* New York: Collier Books, 1973.

Mellor, David, ed. *Germany: The New Photography 1927–33.* London: Arts Council of Great Britain, 1978.

Pollack, Peter. *The Picture History of Photography: From the Earliest Beginnings to the Present Day.* Rev. and enl. ed. New York: Harry N. Abrams, 1969.

MONOGRAPHS

Brockhaus, Christoph, Wolfram Hagspiel, and **Reinhold Misselbeck.** *Werner Mantz: Architekturphotographie in Köln 1926–1932.* Cologne: Museum Ludwig, 1982.

de Vries, Han, and **Peter Hunter-Salomon.** *Erich Salomon: Portrait of an Age.* Translated by Sheila Tobia. 1963 pub. as *Porträt einer Epoche.* New York: Macmillan Company; London: Collier-Macmillan, 1967.

Döblin, Alfred. ''Fotos ohne Unterschrift.'' *Das Kunstwerk* 12 (1946/47): 24–33.

von Hartz, John. *August Sander.* Vol. 7 in *The History of Photography Series.* Millerton, New York: Aperture, 1977.

Hassner, Rune. *Erich Salomon: Unguarded Moments—Images of People, Politics and Society in Europe and USA 1928–1938.* Stockholm: Fotografiska Museet, 1974.

Haus, Andreas. *Moholy-Nagy: Photographs and Photograms.* Trans. Frederic Samson. New York: Pantheon Books; London: Thames and Hudson, 1980.

Hight, Eleanor M., Andrea Kaliski Miller, and **Nancy Nugent.** *Moholy-Nagy: Photography and Film in Weimar Germany.* Wellesley, Massachusetts: Wellesley College Museum, 1985.

Hunter, Peter. *Erich Salomon.* Vol. 10 in *The History of Photography Series.* Millerton, New York: Aperture, 1978.

Honnef, Klaus. *Werner Mantz: Fotografien 1926–1938.* Bonn: Rheinisches Landesmuseum, 1978.

Keller, Ulrich. *August Sander: Menschen des 20. Jahrhunderts: Portraitphotographien 1892–1952.* Ed. Gunther Sander. Munich: Schirmer/Mosel, 1980.

Kempe, Fritz. *Albert Renger-Patzsch: Der Fotograph der Dinge.* Essen: Ruhrland- und Heimatmuseum, 1967.

Kempe, Fritz, and **Carl Georg Heise.** *Albert Renger-Patzsch: 100 Photographs.* Cologne and Boston: Shürmann & Kicken Books, 1979.

Kramer, Robert. *August Sander: Photographs of an Epoch 1904–1959.* Millerton, New York: Aperture, 1980.

Lohse, Bernd, ed. *Hugo Erfurth 1874–1948: Der Fotograf der Goldenen Zwanziger Jahre.* Seebruck am Chiemsee: Heering-Verlag, 1977.

Renger-Patzsch, Albert. *Die Welt ist schön.* Munich: Kurt Wolff Verlag A.G., 1928.

Sander, August, and **Alfred Döblin.** *Antlitz der Zeit: Sechzig Aufnahmen Deutscher Menschen des 20. Jahrhunderts.* 1929. Reprint. Munich: Schirmer/Mosel, 1976.

Sander, August, Gunther Sander, and **Golo Mann.** *Menschen ohne Maske.* Lucerne and Frankfurt: Verlag C.J. Bucher, 1971.

Steinert, Otto, and **G.F. Hartlaub.** *Bildnisse Hugo Erfurth.* Essen: Folkwangschule, 1961.

Thoma, Dieter. *Albert Renger-Patzsch: Ruhrgebiet-Landschaften 1927–1935.* Ed. Ann Wilde and Jürgen Wilde. Cologne: Du Mont Buchverlag, 1982.

Verre, Philip, and **Julie Saul.** *Moholy-Nagy Fotoplastiks: The Bauhaus Years.* New York: The Bronx Museum of the Arts, 1983.